BRITISH
CARS C
1950s AND '60s

James Taylor

SHIRE PUBLICATIONS

Published in Great Britain in 2016 by Shire Publications Ltd, PO Box 883, Oxford, OX1 9PL, UK.

PO Box 3985, New York, NY 10185-3985, USA.

E-mail: shire@shirebooks.co.uk www.shirebooks.co.uk

A CIP catalogue record for this book is available from the British Library.

Shire Library no. 801. ISBN-13: 978 0 74781 432 0

James Taylor has asserted his right under the Copyright, Designs and Patents Act, 1988, to be identified as the author of this book.

Designed by Tony Trucott Designs, Sussex, UK and typeset in Perpetua and Gill Sans.

Printed in China through Worldprint Ltd.

16 17 18   10 9 8 7 6 5 4 3 2

COVER IMAGE
Cover design and photography of Austin-Healey 3000 by Peter Ashley; back cover detail: Triumph TR3 Badge.

TITLE PAGE IMAGE
Interior detail of the Daimler SP250 (see page 43).

CONTENTS PAGE IMAGE
BMC was strongly represented in the sports car market of the 1950s and 1960s, and this line-up at Blenheim Palace shows its 1962 offerings – MG Midget and MGB, and Austin-Healey Sprite and 3000.

ACKNOWLEDGMENTS
Alamy, pages 12, 26, 30–1; British Motor Industry Heritage Centre Limited, pages 3, 4, 7, 9, 10, 14 (both), 15, 16, 17, 18 (both), 19 (both), 21 (upper), 24, 25, 27, 28–9, 31 (upper), 32, 35 (lower), 36 (lower), 38 (both), 39 (both), 41 (upper), 42 (upper), 47, 48, 49, 53, 54 (both); Essex Police, page 36 (upper); Kent Police Museum, page 8; H&H Auctioneers page 21 (lower), 22; Hagertys Auctioneers, page 51 (upper); Historics at Brooklands, pages 1, 20, 23, 43 (lower); Jaguar Land Rover, pages 44–5, 46; Tim Sutton / Sunbeam Alpine Owners' Club, page 33 (all), 51 (lower), 52. All other images from the author's own collection.

Shire Publications is supporting the Woodland Trust, the UK's leading woodland conservation charity, by funding the dedication of trees.

CONTENTS

M G MIDGET

SERIES 'T.C.' TWO-SEATER

Underslung at the rear and upswept over the front axle, the chassis follows the successful line of previous models in the M.G. MIDGET series. Tubular cross-members and box section side members provide a rigidity capable of withstanding the stresses of competition work with a wide margin of strength in hand.

MG·10·9

ORIGINS

THE ORIGINS of the archetypal British sports car of the 1950s and 1960s lie more than two decades earlier, in the 1930s.

Motor sport grew up very early in the history of the automobile, and in the beginning car-makers saw it as a way of attracting publicity and demonstrating their superiority over rival makers. Inevitably, this tended to put the focus on ever larger and more powerful engines, with sizeable cars capable of withstanding the accompanying mechanical stresses. Large and powerful equated to expensive, and that put motor sport out of the reach of all but the very wealthy.

In Britain there was a notable change in the 1920s, when makers began to exploit the desire for sporting performance at an affordable price. Several companies, including Riley (with its 70mph 11/40 Sports Model of 1922) and Alvis (with the 12/40 of the same year that was guaranteed to exceed 60mph), started making lightweight sports models. At a time when the typical family car struggled to manage 50mph, this was high-speed motoring.

It was MG who capitalised on the trend most effectively. Morris Garages had built its first sporting bodies on Morris chassis in 1923 and by the later years of the decade its MG Super Sports, still Morris-based, had become stand-alone models sold under the MG name. In 1928 came a very effective lightweight model called the M-type Midget, built around the chassis and running-gear of the small Morris Minor saloon. This was followed in 1932 by the J-type, which in turn gave way to the P-type of 1934.

These Midgets all had the same basic ingredients. They had minimal open two-seater bodywork, with a rudimentary fabric top and sidescreens to keep out the worst of the British weather. The engines, though based on standard Morris production items, were more highly tuned. Combined with the light weight and small size of the car, they gave sporting performance and nimble handling. Participation in competition by the MG factory helped to develop both these aspects.

Opposite:
The MG TC Midget was really a 1930s car, revised only in detail, but it helped to establish the ground rules for the classic British sports car.

Though car-makers in other European countries were building sports cars to a broadly similar formula, the MG and its rivals remained uniquely British. None of these cars was ever intended for export. Their appeal was that they offered exhilaration at minimal cost. They allowed the wealthy young man of the day to enjoy transport for himself and a friend or girlfriend during the week, with the option of competition in trials or club racing events at weekends.

'The MG is deservedly the most popular small English sports car,' wrote *Motor Sport* magazine in January 1937. By that time, the car had been developed even further. Morris Motors had taken MG under their wing in 1935, and during 1936 had introduced the model that became the definitive small British sports car of the 1930s. This was the T-type Midget, which offered a little more room than the earlier types thanks to a longer wheelbase and a small width increase, but most importantly had a larger engine that gave better performance. *Motor Sport* encapsulated the model's appeal in that same 1937 report:

> Looking back on our test week-end we have pleasant memories of devouring long straight roads at 70 to 80mph, when the engine was really turning over and emitting a truly intriguing roar .... We find it truly difficult to appreciate that the latest Midget sells at £222 and has beneath its lengthy bonnet quite an ordinary push-rod engine ... which gives over 30mpg on normal fast runs .... [the T-type] is in an unassailable position as far as measurable performance is concerned ... the T is not just a polite and gentlemanly edition of former Midgets.

The next important stage in the development of the British sports car was the Second World War and, more importantly, the arrival of the US airmen stationed in Britain from 1942. The MG T-type and other small British sports cars had become popular with airmen of the Royal Air Force, no doubt because they offered the nearest affordable experience to flying on wheels, but also because they had a certain cachet that matched the raffish image RAF officers tended to cultivate at the time. Inevitably, the US airmen came into contact with their British counterparts, and into contact with their cars.

The American domestic car makers had nothing even remotely similar to these lightweight sports cars. American cars tended to be much larger and heavier, with much bigger engines, and agility had simply not been an issue in a country which boasted so many long, straight roads. The performance and fun to be had from these little British sports cars was a revelation, and the US airmen took to them with enthusiasm. When

they went home, they took with them memories of the cars, and in a few cases actually took the cars with them at the end of the war.

The original T-type Midget had become a TB in 1939, and now the company widened the body slightly and revamped it as the TC Midget. Launched in September 1945, the TC Midget was pretty much the car that members of the US 8th Air Force had seen when they were stationed in Britain, and it was the car they wanted to enjoy now they were back home. So did large numbers of other Americans, and the TC Midget sold better than any previous MG of its type in the four years of its production, with particularly strong sales across the Atlantic. No matter that the austere Sir Stafford Cripps, President of the Board of Trade, was busily exhorting British manufacturers to 'export or die' as a way of rebuilding the country's war-torn economy; MG were already doing their bit. When the time came to replace the TC Midget in 1949, MG simply re-engineered the existing model and called it a TD Midget. In the four years of its manufacture, the TD sold 30,000 examples, of which no fewer than 23,488 went to the USA. The TF that replaced the TD in 1953 was very much an evolution of the same design – but by then MG's reliance on a design that recalled the 1930s was out of step with developments elsewhere.

Just one other British car maker achieved export success comparable to that of MG, and this was Jaguar. Always more expensive than the cheap and cheerful MGs, Jaguars – initially marketed as SS-Jaguars – had nevertheless achieved in the 1930s an essentially similar blend of extraordinary value for money and high performance. There were those in the industry who did not like their approach, as they challenged the established makers of performance cars and were often seen as a Johnny-Come-Lately.

'Driving is fun again' – and that was the way US customers saw the little MG. This advertisement hoarding was photographed in California in the late 1940s.

Buying an MG TC in Britain was next to impossible in 1946 unless you were an 'essential user'. The Kent Police qualified for that description, and took delivery of this batch, pictured at MG's Abingdon factory before delivery.

Members of the Jaguar design team had whiled away night-time fire-watching duties at the firm's Coventry factory during the war years by sketching plans for a new engine. Primarily intended for a big saloon car, it was a big six-cylinder twin-cam with a 3.4-litre capacity and power to match the best from makers such as Aston Martin and Bentley. Putting it into a two-seat sports car in 1948 – clothed in an inspired body style which was both simple and yet modern – was a stroke of genius. The new Jaguar XK120 roadster delivered not only wind-in-the-hair motoring for the road but a competition-winning 120mph top speed. It was a sensation, and the US market readily took to it. As home sales were restricted in favour of exports, relatively few Britons got their hands on one until matters eased in the early 1950s.

Not surprisingly, other British car makers cast envious eyes in the direction of the success enjoyed by the MG TC and Jaguar XK120 across the Atlantic, and determined to cash in on this emerging new market. Besides, the government was mercilessly encouraging them to build for export, so there was a powerful incentive to do so. However, most of them failed, for one of two reasons. Some thought they could improve on the raw and frankly rather crude MG by adding refinement and sophistication. This inevitably increased the cost, too. It also missed the point: it was precisely the MG's simplicity and lack of sophistication that lay behind its appeal. Others thought they could improve on the Jaguar's mixture of qualities which, like the MG's, was founded as much on value for money as on anything else. These late 1940s attempts to build volume-selling sports cars served to define what the British sports car was not.

Austin was then the great rival of Morris, which owned the MG marque, and chairman Leonard Lord instructed his designers to come up with an open car that would sell in the USA. However, the new Austin turned out to be a very different kind of vehicle from the MG TC. Its makers tried to design it to meet late 1940s US expectations, and so it had a heavy-looking all-enveloping body with spatted rear wheels, and its size and weight demanded an enlarged 2.6-litre version of the 2199cc four-cylinder engine found in the A70 saloon. Although Austin promoted it heavily, not least with

Jaguar's XK120 was far removed from the MG in appearance, price and performance, yet its essence was the same. This was the two-seat roadster, with few concessions to comfort and every invitation to fun.

a programme of record attempts during 1949, the A90 Atlantic held no real attraction in its intended market. Out of just under 8,000 built, only 350 found US buyers. When Austin and Morris merged to form the British Motor Corporation in 1952, the car disappeared quietly from production.

Triumph was a little more successful. Its 1946 Roadster model was not really intended to tackle the same market as the little MGs. The car was altogether more expensive, and was based on a shortened version of Triumph's new saloon chassis with a body that was inspired by the big Dolomite Roadster of the late 1930s. It tried to be too many things to too many people: not only was there room for three on its bench seat, but two more could be squeezed into a dickey seat in its rounded rear end.

With the 1.8-litre engine from the saloon, it could manage no more than 75mph, a speed which *The Autocar* magazine in 1947 called 'satisfying but not startlingly high'. Fitting the more powerful 2-litre engine from the Standard Vanguard – Standard having bought Triumph at the end of the war

Triumph's interpretation of the roadster – here an 1800 – was once again too sophisticated to attract sports car buyers. The bulbous tail concealed a dickey seat, a feature associated with touring rather than sports models.

– improved the acceleration but had minimal effect on the top speed. Just 2,501 examples of the 1,800 were made, and 2,000 of the 2-litre car. But the Roadster did help Triumph to focus on their next step – one that would strike right into the heart of MG territory.

Meanwhile, makers such as Allard, Alvis and Aston Martin never had any intention of competing directly with the MG T-series Midget, even if they would have welcomed the volume of sales that it achieved.

Sydney Allard had been a small-volume builder of 'specials' in the late 1930s, adding big American engines to lightweight bodies to produce potent competition machines. The car he designed after the war led to a sports model specifically intended for competition, and lacked the cheerful, dual-purpose nature of the MG Midget. The J2 went down well in the USA but was too specialised to achieve big sales and remained a niche car.

Alvis had always aimed high up the market, and believed that it could produce a credible alternative to the Jaguar on the basis of its post-war TA14 saloon chassis. But the TB14 of 1950 was yet another miscalculation. Its 1.9-litre four-cylinder engine took it no faster than 80mph, and it was formidably expensive for a two-seat roadster and had questionable looks. No more than 100 were made before Alvis realised their mistake and stopped production.

Aston Martin was well-established as a maker of sporting machinery before the Second World War, and picked up more or less where it had left off in 1948. Its new car was a two-seat roadster with a 2-litre engine that had been developed during the war. The DB1 was capable of 93mph, but it had two faults. First, the all-enveloping body was simply ugly; and second it did not offer the value-for-money of the new Jaguar XK120. A grand total of 15 were built, which really tells the whole story.

The need to build cars for export rather than for home consumption had been one factor behind the development of the British sports car in the late 1940s; the large and untapped market of North America (primarily the USA) had been another. In these conditions, the outstanding success of MG and Jaguar showed very clearly what was likely to be successful on the world stage, and dictated the way British sports car design would progress in the next decade. Right at the top of the list was excellent value for money, which could perhaps be defined as offering more performance than the price suggested. Next was an element of excitement that came from the configuration: two seats with an open top and minimal weather protection was all that was needed. At this stage, appearance was not a big issue, for although the Jaguar had sleek, all-enveloping bodywork in the modern idiom, the MG still looked like a car designed during the 1930s. Perhaps those who bought the MG were happy to settle for the experience the car brought them, and cared little about the niceties of design.

EXPORT AT ALL COSTS

THERE WAS STILL a desperate irony about Britain in the early 1950s, as MG and Jaguar worked flat out to build their exciting sports cars for export while domestic customers had trouble getting their hands on any sort of new car at all. In 1949, it was estimated that the cars available for British customers that year would meet about one-eighth of the total demand – and of course imports of foreign cars were still subject to government controls and were virtually non-existent. To own an MG TD or a Jaguar XK120 at the start of the decade was an impossible dream for most Britons. Although government restrictions did ease gradually (petrol came off rationing in 1950, for example), it was 1954–5 before buying a new sports car became a realistic proposition for those Britons who could afford one.

Meanwhile, the success of MG and Jaguar in the USA had persuaded other major manufacturers that there was a future in the sports car market. Over the summer of 1952, Sir John Black, Chairman of Standard-Triumph, visited the USA and returned fired up with the idea of building a car to out-do MG in that market. Realising that simplicity was the key to success, he instructed his designers to build a straightforward but modern design around the 2-litre Standard Vanguard engine. Although the prototype car seen on Triumph's stand at the Motor Show in autumn 1952 was some way off the mark, the company took careful note of criticisms and had a redesigned model ready for the Geneva show in March 1953. A specially prepared prototype achieved 124mph in May 1953, and when the new Triumph TR2 went on sale in autumn 1953 it was already highly anticipated.

The headline of the *Autosport* road test of a TR2 in March 1954 said it all: 'World's lowest-priced 100mph sports car is revealed as possessing remarkable acceleration and superb road-holding'. Just a little more expensive than the contemporary MG TF, the new TR2 was some 20mph faster. It was also lower and more modern-looking, with a streamlined full-width body that completely upstaged the MG with its traditional 1930s wings-and-running-boards appearance, and it was entertaining to drive.

Opposite:
The traditional British sports car would never be the same again after the Triumph TR2 arrived in 1952. This is a 1955 car, with the 'short door' configuration introduced when the original full-length doors were found to hit the kerb as they were opened.

Disc wheels made the MG TD look more modern than the TC it replaced; under the skin was a new chassis with independent front suspension and rack-and-pinion steering. This example is seen in the Cotswolds, still rural enough to provide largely traffic-free motoring in the early 1950s.

Creature comforts were sacrificed to performance – there were just two seats, and the soft-top had to be erected laboriously when it rained – but this spartan nature was all part of its appeal. Triumph lost no time in starting exports to the USA, but were hampered by delays, and the TR2 took some time to earn a reputation in its main target market. Meanwhile, Britons were only too pleased to get their hands on the examples that were gradually becoming more freely available on the home market.

Once US exports became established, the Americans loved the new Triumph, especially on the West Coast where the climate was best suited to open cars. *Sports Cars Illustrated* reviewed an example in November 1955 and found that it was 'downright fun to drive' and would give a lot of bigger,

This very British couple, posed in a studio with an MG TF, seem grimly determined to enjoy themselves. The sloping radiator and faired-in headlights did modernise the car a little, but the MG was beginning to look very dated.

There was not much room in the cockpit of a TF, as this picture of a left-hand-drive model shows.

more expensive machines 'a real run for their money and in a lot of instances flatly outdo them.'

Yet it would be wrong to see the TRs as appealing only or even primarily to American buyers. The British loved them, too. On 4 April 1956, *The Motor* magazine described the Triumph TR3 that had just replaced the TR2 as 'extraordinarily suitable for day-to-day motoring of every kind' and wrote that it had performance 'comparable with that of almost any car of less than twice its price' combined with 'roadworthiness of at least a good average sport-car standard, and unusual economy'. The TR's outstanding virtue, however, was deemed to be 'the practical layout which makes it possible for a man to run this as his only car, rather than an occasional and delightful toy.'

The disc-braked TR3A that followed in 1957 – the first mass-produced sports car to have discs – was even better. 'In its latest form the TR3 is an exciting sports car, traditional to drive, fast, flexible and with first-class brakes,' wrote *The Autocar*, and in 1958, noted racing driver Roy Salvadori tried one out for *Autocourse* magazine and reported that the Triumph 'covers the ground at an absurd pace for such a small vehicle and is, more than anything else, responsive. It does whatever you want it to do readily, willingly, with all the rather noisy enthusiasm of a small puppy dog. And it is every bit as likeable.'

The TR3 family remained in production into the 1960s, and it was the Triumph TR range that deserves much of the credit for dragging British sports car design out of the 1930s and into the 1950s. Others soon followed this lead, but the TR series was the original affordable British sports car, and its stripped-down, fun-to-drive nature defined the genre for a generation of buyers. Though it was far from perfect, it was amply good enough. As *The Motor* described the TR3A in 1957, it was 'a design with shortcomings but no vices'.

While Triumph were developing their first car to meet Sir John Black's perceptions of what America wanted, the small independent Donald Healey Motor Company were busily creating a new sports car that they hoped would bring sales success. Founded by a former Triumph engineer, the company had enjoyed some success with its low-volume specialist sports models in the late 1940s, and had designed a new roadster in time for that same 1952 Motor Show where the Triumph was shown. Called the Healey Hundred, it had a modern, sleek and attractive shape and was powered by the 2.6-litre engine from the Austin Atlantic – that miserable failure by Austin to crack the US market.

Leonard Lord, now at the head of the British Motor Corporation, saw the car at the show and immediately recognised its sales potential. On the first day of the exhibition, he persuaded Donald Healey that BMC had the resources to build far more than Healey could in his tiny factory, and a deal was done. Within a year, the new Austin-Healey 100 was on sale, at a

The association between pretty girl and sports car was strong in the 1950s, but to see a girl driving one was the exception. The accepted theory was that the man drove and the girl enjoyed being his passenger. This is a Triumph TR3A, the third evolution of the TR line.

price considerably lower than Healey had proposed, and Austin had begun exports to America.

The new Healey 'looks like the best sports car value to come out of Britain since they repealed the red flag law,' wrote *Autosport* in August 1953. The big engine gave plenty of low-down torque for good acceleration, but that torque also allowed drivers to leave the car in top gear for most of the time and drive it like an automatic. That appealed to US drivers, who were increasingly becoming used to gearboxes that did the driver's work for him. A maximum speed of 110mph was heady stuff for those days, although Donald Healey's claim that his car could match the acceleration of a Jaguar XK120 up to 90mph was a little optimistic. Nevertheless, BMC felt justified in pricing the car much closer to the Jaguar than to its Triumph contemporary.

The car rode comfortably and its two-seat cockpit was quite roomy, while a carefully designed chassis kept scuttle shake to a minimum and made the car an enjoyable drive. If the controls were on the heavy side, this only boosted the Healey's appeal to those whose sports-car tastes went back to pre-war days. The all-drum brakes and basic weather equipment were all part of this appeal. Over a 14-year production run in which the Healey was gradually developed further, more than 90% of those built would be exported to the USA. That was success indeed.

These new designs left MG looking old-fashioned and vulnerable, and by early 1955 they had a new design ready for production. After a fairly successful appearance at that year's Le Mans 24-hour race, the new MGA was announced in September 1955. Low, streamlined, and much prettier than the Triumph which was its obvious rival, the car came initially only as a roadster but was joined by a hardtop coupé model after a year. It was rather slower than the Triumph, but it was cheaper, too.

Sports cars were not just for show. To prove their worth, the major manufacturers entered them in international events, and their stories of success fed the image that survives to this day. Here, the Triumph team for the Tulip Rally in 1958 lines up for a photocall. At the far end of the line is a saloon from Standard, who then owned Triumph.

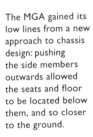

Stereotypical gender roles and the sports car: the girl is the willing passenger and the flat-capped man very obviously the suitably masculine owner in this delightful cameo featuring an MGA.

'To drive the MGA on a winding open road is sheer enthusiast's delight,' said *The Motor* magazine when the car was new. Cornering power was excellent, aided by the very quick rack-and-pinion steering, although the all-drum brakes were close to their limit. Light overall weight allowed the 1.5-litre engine to give excellent performance, although it could certainly be noisy

The MGA gained its low lines from a new approach to chassis design: pushing the side members outwards allowed the seats and floor to be located below them, and so closer to the ground.

under hard acceleration. Above all, the MGA looked modern, and banished forever the 1930s styling associated with the TDs and TFs. It still had its foibles, of course, with sidescreens and soft-top living in a well behind the seats; to raise or lower the hood single-handed was 'an exercise in skill and patience,' reported *The Motor* magazine in an otherwise very favourable review.

A more powerful Twin Cam model arrived in 1958 and benefited from all-round disc brakes as well as extra engine

power, and then an enlarged 1.6-litre pushrod engine became standard for 1959, along with front disc brakes – and improved sidescreens for the roadster models. MGAs went down extremely well in the USA, which took most of those built. Yet despite its relative scarcity in Britain, the MGA was a major part of the sports car scene in the United Kingdom during the second half of the 1950s. It was affordable, it responded to both DIY and specialist tuning, and it was fun. On top of that, international competition successes by the manufacturer's own team lent it huge credibility that undoubtedly had a positive effect on sales.

MG broadened the appeal of the MGA by making a coupé available. The dashboard, as always, was neat and uncluttered. The final models had a 1622cc engine.

19

The two-tone paintwork on this car was more a characteristic of later versions of the Austin-Healey. This, however, is the four-cylinder 100 model. The louvred bonnet was available from Healey, at extra cost, and was also used on the high-performance 100M and 100S models.

By the middle of the 1950s, a hierarchy was apparent among mainstream British sports car makers. It was MG who made the most affordable cars, with Triumph's TR priced just a little bit above them. Some way above that came the Austin-Healey, and then at the top came Jaguar. There were of course several other makers who were trying to find a niche in the market, but most of them were constrained by their resources. Morgan, for example, built some very credible machines to what was essentially a pre-war design, but made them by hand and to order. Aston Martin, which again relied on small-volume manufacture, had a formidable reputation but catered only for the very top of the market and in real terms offered little that Jaguar could not, except for exclusivity.

There was a further irony at work by the middle of the decade. While it was Americans who bought the majority of British sports cars and loved them for their uncompromising nature as well as their unashamed fun element, it was also Americans who gradually pushed British manufacturers to embrace change. In January 1956, a journalist for *Motor Trend* magazine directed a few well-chosen words at the makers of British sports cars in general. 'I hope that they will soon recognise the fact that performance (and more particularly, acceleration) is what the majority of the American motoring public desires,' he wrote. It was not amusing to be driving a supposedly sporting MGA, as in this instance, and to be seen off at every traffic-lights Grand Prix by a standard domestic US saloon.

Despite the modern appearance of the Austin-Healey, weather protection was still rudimentary. This close-up shows the sidescreen of a 1954 model; the flap at the bottom allowed the hand signals which were still very much a feature of motoring.

But those American buyers did not just want more performance. They also wanted more creature comforts – or at least, US dealers who handled British sports cars thought they did. The hardy nature of the archetypal British sports car was seen as a deterrent to wider sales, and so the makers obliged by adding comfort, refinement and new features.

When Jaguar built on the success of their original XK120 with the XK140 in 1954, the new car was no faster. Instead, its engine had been moved forwards to help make room for an occasional rear seat – or, in the two-seater roadster, to give more fore-and-aft adjustment of the seats. When XK140 became XK150 in 1957, its all-disc brakes were a long-overdue improvement, but perhaps more telling was that the roadgoing competition car feel of the original XK had been replaced by a grand touring bias. The interior boasted more leather trim and the seats were more comfortable still.

When Triumph replaced their original TR2 with the broadly similar TR3 in 1955, they made room for an occasional rear seat and increased the

Aston Martin's strength lay in expensive grand-touring coupés, but it had a formidable sporting heritage. This is a 1956 DB2/4 Vantage convertible, too grand and too rare to qualify as an archetypal British sports car despite sharing much of the spirit of the breed.

Jaguar had gradually developed its XK range during the 1950s, and by the end of the decade the top model was the XK150S, with triple-carburettor 3.8-litre engine and 135mph performance. The car offered more cockpit room than its predecessors, but had also put on weight.

range of optional extras. When the Austin-Healey went to a new model in 1956, it gained a smoother six-cylinder engine and a cut-back rear deck to allow for two occasional rear seats. That these improvements were the formula for success was indisputable. Sales figures of British sports cars just kept on climbing – except in the odd year of economic recession – and although there were some exports to other countries, the focus remained firmly on the USA.

Nearly 92,500 MGAs were built in the six years from 1955 to 1961, and of those fewer than 6,000 were sold in Britain. In the same period, Triumph built more than 71,500 TR3s and TR3As, of which fewer than 5,500 went to UK buyers. As already noted, more than 90% of all the Austin-Healeys built between 1953 and 1967 went to America, and the production bias of Jaguar XKs (25,224 with left-hand drive out of 30,504 between 1948 and 1961) makes clear where Jaguar had aimed their sights.

Undeniably, it was Austin-Healey, Triumph and MG who established the pattern for mass-produced British sports cars in the 1950s, with Jaguar providing the more expensive models that were just out of the financial reach of the everyday buyer. That pattern relied on a number of factors – and the elements that had made up the successful British sports car of the late 1940s were still prevalent in the mix.

The typical successful British sports car of the 1950s was a roadster, offering two seats or two seats plus a token rear seat suitable only for small children. It also offered good value for money; buyers and magazine professionals alike tended to evaluate the worth of these cars on how much performance per pound they offered.

Another key factor was that the British sports car could be used not only for fun at weekends (and many were indeed thrashed mercilessly round race tracks at club events both in Europe and the USA) but was also a thoroughly practical proposition as everyday transport. Sporting successes by the manufacturers' teams in events such as the Le Mans 24 Hours and the SCCA Championships in the USA provided the backdrop and added an element of excitement.

The driving enjoyment expected of these cars was not purely derived from their performance and handling. A lot of it had to do with the way they drove: buyers liked what was often described as a 'vintage' feel, in which man had to master machine and was not cosseted while he did so. A baulky gearshift or a tendency to oversteer at the limit were not seen as disadvantages but more as character, although cars that suffered from terminal handling problems or vague gearchanges were not tolerated. The sensation of speed in an open body was just as important as it had been in the cars of the previous decade.

On top of that, it was a bonus if a car was simple enough to be maintained by its enthusiastic owner and could be tuned and modified to improve its performance. A large specialist industry grew up to encourage this aspect

TVR was another small company, whose first car was the Grantura of 1958. As the name suggests, it was as much touring car as sports car. It could be bought fully assembled or as a kit of parts into which the buyer put his own choice of engine. All were coupés with glass-fibre bodies.

of ownership, offering everything from open-backed 'racing' gloves to multiple-carburettor conversions.

All of this is thrown into sharp relief by a look at some of the British sports cars that failed to make the grade. There were many small companies that were born out of enthusiasm and always remained far too small to cater for the mass market; meanwhile Lotus, later to become a significant player, was in this period very much a small-volume specialist maker. But there were other entries into the sports-car market, made by big companies with big resources, and these turned out to be failures.

One example was the cars from Sunbeam, one of several marques owned by the Rootes Group. Sunbeam had a strong sporting heritage, and from 1948 marketed a range of attractive sports saloons and drophead coupés under the Sunbeam-Talbot name. The company announced a more powerful two-seat roadster derivative in 1953, the Sunbeam Alpine. But it was too big, too heavy, and too dated in its styling to convince, although it did score some notable rally successes. The Alpine was not listed after October 1955, by which time approximately 3,000 had been made.

Another also-ran of the period was Daimler. The company had never been known as a maker of sports cars, but it tried its hand in 1953 with a model called the Century Roadster. Though it was indeed a roadster in concept, it was far too big, heavy and grand to suit the taste of the times, and Daimler gave up on it after building just 65 examples, revamping it as a drop-head coupé in 1955; that fell flat too, with only 54 being made.

The Swallow Doretti made only a brief impact on the sports car market in 1954–5. It used an advanced tubular chassis with a Triumph TR engine, but its price was nearly 25% higher than that of the Triumph.

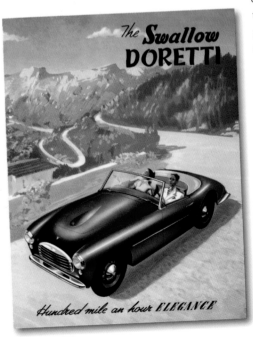

Lastly, the Singer Nine deserves a mention if only for its failure to keep up with the times. Still an independent company (although it would be absorbed into the Rootes Group in 1956), Singer revitalised its Nine roadster in 1945. This was a 1939 design that was simply warmed-over to give the company an exportable product, and it remained pre-war in looks and behaviour even after being transformed into the bigger-engined SM Roadster in 1951. This was not available in Britain until 1953, by which time it had been overtaken by events. Without the performance or the modernity of the latest British sports roadsters, it disappeared in 1955.

NEW CARS FOR NEW TIMES

IT BECAME quite apparent as the 1950s wore on that Britain's car manufacturers were not catering for every corner of the sports car market. Their pursuit of export sales had led them to make cars that were too big and too expensive for many of the young enthusiasts who wanted sports cars, and that enthusiasm had found its own outlet in a demand for cars built from kits. These kits – packages of parts that the buyer assembled into a complete car – catered for the hands-on, do-it-yourself enthusiast and were also exempt from Purchase Tax, which brought costs right down. Those who built them could choose to fit low-cost second-hand parts (such as engines and gearboxes) which reduced the cost even further.

It was BMC who first saw a way to make money from this market. They invited the Donald Healey Motor Company to design a sports car using as

The Austin-Healey Sprite injected a new affordability into the sports car market at the end of the 1950s. This is the original 'Frogeye' model whose headlamps contributed a great deal to its cheeky charm.

BMC created the Austin-Healey marque, and also owned MG. When MG wanted a small sports car, the Austin-Healey Sprite was 'badge-engineered' to become an MG Midget, and the Sprite took on the same new look. Among the improvements were a proper boot. This MG was exported to Nova Scotia, Canada.

many components as possible from their existing Austin A35 and Morris Minor small saloons. The aim was to produce a really cheap sports car that would provide enjoyable motoring, and by May 1958 the new car was ready. It was called the Austin-Healey Sprite and became the first mass-produced sports car to swap separate-chassis construction for a unitary body shell.

The Sprite was incredibly cheap. At £445 before Purchase Tax when launched, it was a little over half the £817 price of the bigger Healey, and it was around two-thirds of the price of BMC's own MGA at £663. For that price, buyers had to manage without external access to the boot (the seat back folded down to give access from inside) and with a strictly two-seat cockpit whose weather protection was stowed in the boot: if it rained, the hood and sidescreens had to be extracted and then erected, as fast as possible. There were drum brakes all round and the quarter-elliptic rear suspension could make cornering rather interesting, although it was safe enough to feel like fun.

Fun was the reason for the Sprite's existence. It was not particularly fast, although it was small and low enough to feel a lot faster than it really was from inside the tiny cockpit. 'The car is specifically intended to provide enjoyable, sporting motoring at low cost,' wrote *The Autocar* in June 1958. 'While acceleration and speed at first glance seem modest, the character, behaviour, economy of operation and, not least, the low initial cost combine to make a very rewarding total.'

DIY enthusiasts loved the superb engine accessibility from a one-piece front end combining bonnet and wings, and the poor weather protection simply added to the traditional British sports-car appeal of enjoyable hardship. The car's cheeky looks added immeasurably to its appeal, with headlamps perched in pods on top of the bonnet; British buyers called it the Frogeye, while Americans knew it as the Bug-eye.

However, the original design lasted only until 1961. The car was already being built at the MG factory in Abingdon, and not surprisingly the MG people wanted a slice of its success. In May 1961 the Sprite was restyled, with a more orthodox front and a restyled rear with an opening boot. A month later it was joined by an MG Midget clone, priced exactly £10 higher before Purchase Tax. Between them, these redesigns anticipated the shape of the new medium-sized MG that would arrive a year later.

However, the Sprite and Midget did not have things their own way for very long. Triumph had seen the same market opportunity, and after their 1961 takeover by truck-maker Leyland they finally had the resources to push forward with their own contender. When the Triumph Spitfire was announced in 1962, it moved the small sports car on quite dramatically.

Although the Spitfire was based on a traditional separate chassis (that of Triumph's small Herald saloon), it had disc brakes on the front wheels, independent rear suspension, and a slightly larger engine than the BMC cars. A hinged front end made engine accessibility just as good as on the original Sprite, and the body drawn up by Italian stylist Michelotti was infinitely prettier than any Sprite or Midget. It was still crude in many ways, with a build-it-yourself soft top, rubber mats on the floor, and a heater only at extra cost, but it did have winding windows and a boot with external

Overleaf: Both Sprite and Midget remained available for the rest of the 1960s, with only cosmetic differences between the two. This 1968 publicity picture of a Sprite makes clear they were intended for young owners – and this one has already managed to lose the cover for the jacking point below the windscreen pillar.

Introduced in 1964, alongside the largely identical Sprite MkIII, the MG Midget MkII gained wind-up windows and semi-elliptic rear springs.

access. *The Motor* reported in November 1962 that the Spitfire's trim 'verges on the spartan... the effect inside the car (perhaps not inappropriately in a sports car) is of everything being made highly resistant to wear, wind and weather'.

For this new model, which *The Motor* said would appeal 'equally as a comfortable road car and useful competition mount,' Triumph charged a little more than BMC were asking for their small sports models. Before Purchase Tax was added, the prices in October 1962 were £485 for the Sprite, £495 for the Midget, and £530 for the Spitfire. None of that deterred the buyers: in the two years from 1962 to 1964, BMC sold 11,215 Sprites and 9,601 Midgets, averaging around 10,400 a year, while in the three years from 1962 to 1965, Triumph sold 45,733 Spitfires for an average of more than 15,200 a year.

BMC fought back, of course. Their Sprites and Midgets received a larger 1098cc engine from 1962 to compete more effectively with the 1147cc

Below: Not to be outdone by the small BMC sports cars, Triumph introduced its Spitfire in 1962.

Left: The Spitfire was a car docile enough to attract women drivers as well as men, and it could even double as practical family transport. That was the message of this publicity picture, taken at a time when the second car was an emerging phenomenon in Britain. The car is a MkII model.

Let us not forget that the Spitfire was also intended to earn American dollars, and it did so very effectively. This transporter-load of MkII models were all intended for US customers.

Spitfire. BMC and Triumph would jockey for position at this end of the sports-car market right through the 1960s: Sprites and Midgets were given wind-up windows in 1964 and went to 1275cc and a permanently fitted soft-top in 1966, so the following year Spitfires went to 1296cc and gained a similarly fitted soft-top.

Spitfires out-sold the combined Sprite and Midget models every year except 1969, when Spitfire production was restricted by a strike. Meanwhile, enthusiasm for kit-cars in Britain diminished, and the new small sports models from the British 'majors' proved a big success across the Atlantic, where American buyers welcomed this new breed of affordable fun car. Exports remained vital to the manufacturers' balance sheets, and around two-thirds of all the Spitfires built in the 1960s were sold overseas.

THE MAINSTREAM

Under the impact of the new cheaper sports cars, the successors to the mainstream sports cars of the 1950s created a new medium-sized class for the 1960s. Price was again a defining characteristic. In 1960, these cars in their roadster forms were all priced before Purchase Tax at between £660 and £700, and by 1968 those prices were between £965 and £1000. Engine sizes and types were important, too, and all these cars had four-cylinder engines of between 1500cc and 2200cc. Front disc brakes were expected, together with a respectable soft-top for weather protection, and either a

Sunbeam was the sporting marque of the Rootes Group, who determined to get their share of the medium-sized sports car market with the new Alpine. The sharp fin-like rear wings were inspired by American design trends, and were expected to appeal to US and domestic buyers alike.

Sunbeam recognised the need to keep its Alpine competitive, and gave it a larger engine after just one year in production.

SUNBEAM ALPINE
now with larger 1·6 litre engine

The Alpine's fins were toned down after a few years, and for 1964 Sunbeam introduced an automatic gearbox option. It did not prove popular, however.

Opposite: Triumph's TR4 was recognisably a member of the TR family but came with a much more modern look for the 1960s and winding windows instead of sidescreens.

detachable hardtop option or an alternative closed body style. Overdrive was not an essential, but was usually an extra-cost option.

The USA was still the key market, and its tastes still played a major part in defining these cars. As in the 1950s, the big players were MG and Triumph, but from 1959 they were joined by a third maker. This was the Rootes Group, whose earlier Sunbeam Alpine roadster had been something of a sales flop. With their eyes firmly fixed on US sales, in 1959 Rootes announced a new open two-seater Sunbeam as a direct competitor for the MGA and Triumph TR3A, and resurrected the old Alpine name.

As a product, the Alpine followed the traditional recipe of drawing on existing saloon production components. But its monocoque design was more modern than either of its rivals, and its dart-like shape was quite different, incorporating relatively restrained tail fins that were inspired by contemporary US styling trends. Typical of Rootes products, which were generally better equipped than their rivals, it had the winding windows that they lacked and its soft top was attached to the body and did not have to be fished out of the boot when the weather turned inclement. There was a proper heater, too, and the whole car was rather softer and more civilised than its direct rivals.

Writer Richard Langworth quoted a description of the Alpine as 'a tasty car, which the young man was bought by his Daddy', and it certainly did have a slightly more up-market and respectable image than its rivals. It was rather slower than the contemporary Triumph, though still capable of 100mph, and despite its relative sophistication it had enough of what the customers expected. For US journalist Tom McCahill, writing in *Mechanix Illustrated*, it was not 'the greatest sports car I've ever twirled down the pike, but at $2599 it's the best offering dollar-for-dollar since the first Austin-Healey hit here in the early '50s.'

Expectations in the sports-car market were clearly changing, and when Triumph introduced their new TR4 in 1961, the car had moved on in many

Between 1961 and 1963 the Alpine could be given this remarkable hardtop coupé conversion by coachbuilder Harrington. The Alpine name was not used, and the car was called a Sunbeam Harrington Le Mans – the Le Mans part coming from an Alpine's success in the Index of Thermal Efficiency at the famous 24-hour race.

areas. Though it was still built in the traditional way with a separate chassis, it had a sleeker, less rounded body shape from the drawing-board of Italian designer Michelotti – and even had traces of the tail fins that US customers liked, as well as incorporating a bigger boot. There was a striking new style of optional hardtop called a Surrey top, with a detachable roof section.

The TR4 was fast enough to make a useful police pursuit car. This one is pictured at Southend in Essex.

With the TR4A came independent rear suspension – an advanced feature for the time but one compromised by it being grafted onto the existing chassis.

winding windows in full-height doors, front disc brakes, rack-and-pinion steering and an all-synchromesh gearbox dragged the TR into the new era of the 1960s. There was a bigger engine, too.

At this point, the dead weight of US customer tastes became very apparent. 'Almost immediately,' reported *Sports Car World* magazine in

October 1963, 'there were people saying that the TR series was no longer a sports car and that American comfort-seekers had managed to convert [sic] good old English know-how and design.'

MG were the last to catch up with the latest trends, when they launched their MGB to replace the MGA in 1962. Carefully pitched just below the TR4 in price, the new car had a smaller engine, too, although at 1798cc it had grown

slightly from the 1622cc of the MGA. This bigger engine, said *Autocar* in September 1962, had been introduced 'to give the extra power which North American buyers expect of this size of sports car.'

Unlike the TR4, the MGB used a modern monocoque structure. It now had the disc brakes and winding windows that rivals had led buyers to expect, and although its soft-top was detachable as standard, for extra cost it could be permanently attached to the body. This was not quite as much of an advantage as it sounded. *The Motor* magazine in September 1962 reported, with characteristically British understatement, that it could not be said that raising and lowering the hood were simply the 'work of a moment' and if the driver were alone he would be involved in 'quite a battle, and a succession of trips from one side to the other, to convert the car from the open or closed condition.'

Such shortcomings apart, the MGB was precisely on target. Nimble, affordable, good-looking and modern in concept, it still had enough of the

Not to be outdone by the Sunbeam Harrington Le Mans, Triumph dealer Dove's of Wimbledon commissioned the same coachbuilder to build a similar conversion for the TR4. Though rare, it anticipated the market that MG would later pick up with the MGB GT. It continued into the era of the TR4A, of which this is an example.

MG replaced the MGA with the MGB in 1962, and the 'B' went on to become the most-sold British sports car of the period. This overhead view of a 1962 car shows that the cockpit was far more roomy than the T-type models of ten years earlier. The studio shot of a 1965 car shows the well-judged lines and the resemblance to the contemporary Midget and Sprite.

rawness that buyers on both sides of the Atlantic wanted. The car rapidly seized the initiative from Triumph's TR series, and in the five years between 1962 and 1967 nearly 116,000 of the roadster variant found buyers; in the six years between 1961 and 1967, Triumph sold just under 68,800 of the TR4 and its TR4A successor.

Though the MGB roadster could be bought with a removable hardtop at extra cost, BMC realised that there was more to be had from the basic design. So from 1965 they introduced a sister model called the MGB GT, which had a strikingly attractive fixed-roof fastback body. This incorporated a bench rear seat, and even though legroom was severely restricted, it made the car altogether more viable for those with a young family. *Motor* magazine's verdict in February 1966 was typical:

The vintage aspect of the MG character has not been lost: there is a purposeful clatter when starting up; the steering is direct and feels very positive (though rather heavy) in the best vintage way; and the straight-cut bottom gear emits a loud whine ... Many 'elderly' ex-MG owners will be tempted to throw off their marital saloon car chains.

Despite the advance of modern technology, it was clear that a proper sports car was better if it was not too sophisticated, and the MGB GT hit exactly the right note. Over the next six years, to mid-1971, it found more than 113,000 buyers – who were additional to those for the roadster models. Not for nothing is the MGB now seen as the archetypal British sports car of the 1960s.

Sunbeam, meanwhile, had been busily improving their Alpine sports model. They responded to customer feedback by raising the steering wheel to give more legroom, modifying the window channels to stop rattles, and improving performance with a bigger engine. From 1963, the Alpine also boasted an 11-cubic-foot boot, giving it more luggage space than any other sports car of the time. From 1964 the tail-fins were toned down and – a first in this class – an automatic gearbox option was introduced; for 1965 the manual gearbox gained synchromesh on first gear.

From 1965, a further enlarged engine brought 100mph within reach, but none of these changes made the Alpine a best-seller. It sold rather over

The MGB GT was Abingdon's attempt to make the sports car family-friendly. It followed the similar small-volume attempts by Harrington, but was a purpose-built car rather than a conversion, using a taller integral windscreen instead of the MGB roadster's shallow bolt-on screen. This is a 1968 example.

However, a lot depended on the size of the family; there was not a lot of room in the MGB GT's fold-flat rear seats.

69,000 examples in nine years (so averaging just under 7,700 a year), which was nowhere near the levels achieved by MG and Triumph. Production ended in 1968 when new crash-safety regulations in the USA would have demanded a major redesign to relocate the twin fuel tanks then mounted in the rear wings.

Triumph, too, had been busy. They improved their TR4 in 1964 by adding an independent rear suspension, a development more or less forced on them by the fact that their own cheaper Spitfire model already had such a system. Though it improved both the ride and – to a limited degree – the handling, it was not universally liked. When Triumph showed the new TR4A to their US dealers, one major importer was adamant that US customers would not be prepared to pay the higher price that the new suspension demanded, and would probably not appreciate the benefits it brought; consequently Triumph hastily prepared a special TR4A for the USA, with the older style of live rear axle. Somewhat taken aback, and recognising that they were losing the sales battle to the MGB, Triumph changed tack for the next generation of TR, moving it subtly into the more expensive category occupied by sports cars with multi-cylinder engines.

MORE CYLINDERS, MORE REFINEMENT

The top level of British sports cars in the 1960s was largely defined by cost. In 1960, the dividing line stood at around £800 before Purchase Tax was added. By 1964, that dividing line stood at around £900, and by 1968 it was just under the £1,000 mark, again before tax was added. For comparison, an imported Ferrari was around £4,500 before tax in 1960, and the cheapest in 1968 was around £5,500. (The percentage of Purchase Tax that the government levied changed several times during the 1960s, and car makers loved to quote the untaxed figure, which made their products sound less expensive. In reality, Purchase Tax added a substantial amount to the quoted prices.)

For these higher asking prices, buyers of British sports cars expected a number of things not available on cheaper models. Most important was a multi-cylinder engine. Along with that, they expected at least the option of an overdrive to make the car viable as a long-distance tourer; and for long-distance touring they expected higher levels of refinement, comfort and equipment than they could find in lower-priced models.

The main contenders at the start of the 1960s came from BMC, Jaguar and – a surprise new entrant to the market – Daimler. It was the Austin-Healey that flew the flag for BMC in this market, newly up-engined during 1959 with a 3-litre 'six' to become the Austin-Healey 3000. The car's basic design, of course, went back to the early 1950s and was by now beginning to date. Sliding Perspex sidescreens (to be abandoned in 1962) and heavy

Austin Healey 3000

2-SEATER AND OCCASIONAL 4-SEATER
SPORTS CARS

controls helped give it a distinctive image as a he-man's car, and that image helped the car sell in spite of its shortcomings. These included poor cockpit ventilation, poor ground clearance, and a small fuel tank which restricted range unacceptably for a long-distance tourer.

Front disc brakes made it a little more modern, and the addition of an optional brake servo in 1961 helped. Yet the Big Healey undeniably had character. John Bolster of *Autosport* was impressed by 'the sheer power of the big engine', and wrote that this feeling endured after hundreds of miles of driving. The Austin-Healey 3000, he said, was 'a wonderfully effortless car.' Over in the USA, where the vast majority of Healey 3000s were sold, *Car and Driver*

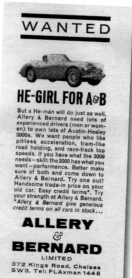

The Austin-Healey 3000 cultivated an image as a he-man's car. This is a MkI, with the same 'crinkle-cut' grille as the preceding 100-Six.

London dealers Allery & Bernard would have been quite happy to find 'he-girls' among their customers in 1964, although most buyers were certainly men.

Though the Big Healey was an expensive car with a six-cylinder engine, it was still sparsely equipped, at least in the early 1960s. This MkII model shows the token rear seat and the absence of a permanently fitted soft-top – a failing rectified on the later cars.

More power for the MkIII version of the Big Healey took top speed up to 125mph, making it 'the fastest sports car you can own for less than £1500' according to this February 1964 advertisement. The MkIII – and the preceding MkIIa – also had an integral hood, visible here under its neat cover.

said that 'the ponderous nature of all the controls is a factor which lends a kind of appealing masculinity to the car ... harking back to the days when men were men.'

The USA had been Daimler's main target when they had announced their new sports car in 1959; the venue chosen had been the New York Show. Daimler was best known for its grand limousines, and the arrival of a sports car after the failure of the Century Roadster in the mid-1950s was a major surprise to buyers and industry insiders alike. But Daimler was in trouble, needed a big-selling product quickly, and decided to risk entering what it saw as a seller's market.

Being a Daimler, the new SP250 (which was to have been called the Dart until Dodge objected) was pitched high up the market, between the Healey 3000 and the Jaguars. It was also very different from other models in its class, with a brand-new 2.5-litre V8 engine and a body made of glass-fibre – the former being a real jewel and the latter resulting from a need to save tooling costs. Winding windows, a luxuriously trimmed interior with a small rear bench seat, all-disc

Austin Healey changes up!

All the way up to a faster, more comfortable, new 3000 Mark III!

brakes and a decent-sized boot all made this a very special proposition. Better yet, it offered the option of an automatic gearbox, which no rivals did in 1959.

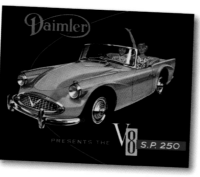

Daimler's SP250 was a surprise entry at the top end of the sports car class. Its V8 engine was a delight, although the glass-fibre bodywork took some time to get right, and the styling was an acquired taste.

Unfortunately, its shape was little short of bizarre, partly thanks to tail fins of the type popularised on American cars in the 1950s. Its chassis was also rather crude, and the new gearbox was poor. Then there were build quality problems. 'It is common knowledge that the earlier models were not altogether satisfactory, chiefly because the glass-fibre body work was crude in the extreme and such dire happenings as doors flying open while the car was being driven fast did nothing to enhance the reputation of the new Daimler,' wrote *Motor Sport* in May 1961.

By the time that was written, the SP250 story was as good as over. Daimler had sold out to Jaguar in May 1960, and Jaguar did not need any in-house competition for their own sports cars. Though they made some rapid changes to stiffen the body and improve the chassis, plans for a restyled model foundered, and the last SP250s were made in 1964.

This later SP250 was one of several bought for pursuit duties by London's Metropolitan Police. It had an automatic gearbox, one of the options that Daimler pioneered in the sports car market.

Previous page and Above: In 1961, Jaguar replaced its XK range with the stunning E-type – known as an XK-E in the USA, where the XK name had a strong pull. It was claimed to be good for 150mph (although needing special preparation to achieve that) and was a real show-stopper; even Enzo Ferrari described it as 'the most beautiful car in the world'. In some people's eyes it looked best as a roadster, but the fixed-head coupé proved more popular in rainy Britain.

Jaguar themselves entered the 1960s with the XK150 and quicker XK150S, but these would not remain available for long. From 1961 they were replaced by the E-type (XK-E in the USA, where most were sold). This was a simply astonishing cocktail of good looks and high performance at an unbeatable price. *The Motor* wrote on 22 March 1961 of its 'elegance of line... allied to a combination of performance, handling and refinement that has never been equalled at the price and, we would think, very seldom surpassed at any price.'

Simply put, the E-type raised the game for every maker of sports cars. Its performance (150mph was promised straight off the showroom floor, although a little optimistically) worried Aston Martin whose cars cost nearly twice as much, and did the same to Ferrari, whose prices were another 50% higher in Britain. The E-type was far from flawless, of course, and the brakes on early cars were distinctly under par, while cockpit room was limited. But Jaguar could hardly make enough to meet demand, and quickly improved the car with a bigger engine and better brakes among other things. The E-type went on to become a legend in its own right, and remains the talismanic British sports car of the 1960s.

Jaguar took a further decisive step in 1966, introducing a longer-wheelbase fixed-roof model with 2+2 seating. It was, admittedly, not as pretty as the original coupé, which remained available, but it broadened the market and its automatic gearbox option hinted at another new trend in British sports cars. The extra nine inches of length in the cabin were allied to a higher roof, and *Motor* underlined its appeal in its report of 30 April 1966. 'You can now have an E-type for six-footers who can also extend the ownership for at least seven years of family ties, or more with a family of one trained to sit transversely,' wrote the magazine, whilst admitting that two adults would be 'decidedly uncomfortable' in the occasional rear seat. If the E-type 2+2 had made the quality sports car a more practical proposition for the enthusiast with a young family, it had not quite bridged the gap between young adulthood and the requirements of the middle-aged enthusiast.

Meanwhile, the appeal of a six-cylinder engine had encouraged Triumph to launch a new model that considerably undercut on price any other British sports car with a multi-cylinder engine. This was the GT6, which combined the essence of the Spitfire with a closed fastback body derived from the company's recent Le Mans racers and the compact 2-litre engine from their saloon range. Though the car had only two seats, a Triumph spokesman told *Motor* magazine of 15 October 1966 that 'we don't mind comparisons with a miniature E-type or Aston Martin'.

In practice, the car's real rival was the MGB GT, and the GT6's competitive edge came from its six-cylinder engine and its better performance. Though the Americans liked it – 'an extremely good car, much improved over any previous Triumph offering,' said *Car and Driver* in May 1967 – the truth was that it was cramped inside and suffered from poor cabin ventilation. The rear suspension was also a serious weakness that gave the car unpredictable handling. Although a redesign cured this from 1968, the damage had been done and the GT6 never quite gained the place in buyers' affections that its basic concept deserved.

Triumph brought the entry price for six-cylinder sports cars right down with its GT6, derived from the Spitfire and the related Vitesse saloon. It was only ever available as a coupé.

Triumph also upgraded its TR range in October 1967 by making the new TR5 a six-cylinder car. Its engine was half a litre larger than that in the GT6, but made the car little quicker than the TR4A it replaced. That it was a TR counted in its favour; that it became more expensive in the process did not, and the TR5 sat uncomfortably astride the medium and upper categories for its two-year production run. In Britain it had petrol injection, but emissions-control and cost concerns persuaded Triumph to sell it across the Atlantic as a carburettor-engined TR250. With few other improvements to recommend it, the Americans saw it as rather old-fashioned – and nobody liked the fake-Rostyle wheel trims that concealed plain steel disc wheels.

The trend towards multi-cylinder engines perhaps reached its nadir with the MGC, which was announced at the same time as the TR5. Essentially, it was BMC's replacement for the Big Healey that had gone out of production a year earlier. The search for production economies led quite logically to a decision that the car should use the existing structure of the MGB (then only six years old) and should have the latest version of the BMC 3-litre six-cylinder engine.

The TR range took on a six-cylinder engine when the TR5 arrived. The profusion of badges reminded onlookers that this was a 2.5-litre engine, too – much smaller than the Jaguar's 4.2 litres but also much larger than the 1.8 litres of a four-cylinder MGB.

Unfortunately, the new engine turned out heavier than planned, and fatally compromised the car's handling as well as delivering less performance than its size promised. An optional automatic gearbox followed the thinking that had seen Jaguar offer one for its 2+2 E-type, but did nothing for the performance. A slow start to production did not help, and the cars were almost unavailable until 1968. Lack of interest saw the MGC disappear in September 1969, after just two years. Perhaps it looked too much like the cheaper MGB to persuade buyers; perhaps it lacked the character of the Big Healey it replaced; equally perhaps its perceived handling shortcomings were a deterrent. As John Bolster had it in *Autosport*, 'the understeer rather discourages one from chancing an unknown corner at an optimistic speed'.

One last car in this price category is worthy of mention, and that is the Lotus Elan. In many ways, this car exemplified the British sports car of the 1960s just as much as Jaguar's E-type. The fact that British Purchase Tax did not apply to kit cars persuaded Lotus to export the Elan in kit form in 1962, until the tax rules changed and the cars could be imported fully built. Even in kit form, it was expensive – the 1962 price of £1,090 was only £100 less than that of a Big Healey complete with Purchase Tax. That made it very much an enthusiast's car.

BMC tried to replace the Big Healey with a six-cylinder version of the MGB, called the MGC. Unfortunately, it was not a success. This car, pictured at Henley-on-Thames, shows the distinctive bonnet bulge of the 'C'.

The Lotus Elan was priced to compete with the multi-cylinder cars, but was really in a class of its own. Lightweight, fast and with a mix of excellent roadholding and a supple ride, the Elan marked a coming-of-age for Lotus.

The Elan could hardly have been less like the Healey. It was a lightweight two-seater with a technically advanced backbone frame, a glass-fibre body, all-independent suspension, all-disc brakes and a 1.6-litre four-cylinder twin-cam engine derived from racing experience. Though details were crude – the windows on early cars slid up and down and often refused to stay up – its handling was unsurpassed, and *Motor* magazine had no qualms about calling the car 'the ultimate in its chosen field' in 1964. Sales were never huge, but Lotus kept on improving the Elan throughout the

1960s and the car retained its charm to the end. From 1967 it was joined by a lengthened Elan +2 that followed Jaguar's E-type 2+2 example with a lengthened wheelbase and room for a (very small) family. Once again, the model appealed to hardcore enthusiasts, but the Elan is today fondly remembered as a key part of the 1960s British sports car legend.

The four-cylinder Morgan was a 1930s design at heart, but was well priced. The basic design was retained when Morgan entered the multi-cylinder class in 1968 with the Plus 8 that featured a Rover 3.5-litre V8 engine.

AC and Sunbeam up-engined their existing models with an American-made V8, although these cars were never very big sellers. The AC Cobra and Sunbeam's Alpine-derived Tiger used the same US-sourced 'small bloe' V8, the Cobra later going on to even bigger engines.

WHAT WENT WRONG?

A cutaway of the original Sunbeam Alpine, with its fuel tank below the boot floor. In 1963 twin tanks were fitted in the wings, to allow more boot space. Re-engineering to meet late 1960s US legislation was considered too expensive, and the Alpine was withdrawn.

THE PACE OF CHANGE in British sports-car design between the late 1940s and the end of the 1960s had been quite glacial. All-enveloping bodies had replaced the wings-and-running-boards designs, and a proper folding hood, winding windows, disc brakes, overdrive and independent rear suspension had gradually found their place. But the qualities of rawness and excitement that had characterised the breed at the start of that period were still present nearly a quarter of a century later. Yet towards the end of that period there were already clear signs of a different future. Outside influences had begun to accelerate the pace of change, and by the start of the 1970s the British sports car industry was struggling to keep up.

Those changes had begun in the middle of the 1960s, as the British motor industry had embarked on a period of mergers and takeovers. The American Chrysler company gradually took control of the Rootes Group after 1964; BMC acquired Jaguar in 1966 and became British

Motor Holdings; and in 1968 British Motor Holdings itself merged with the Leyland Motor Corporation (which already owned Standard-Triumph) to become the British Leyland Motor Corporation.

One very important result was that formerly rival companies MG and Triumph found themselves obliged to work together. But the company loyalties and cultures that had been built up over many decades were not so easily dismissed, and co-operation was not so easily achieved. As these internal conflicts worked themselves out, some marques disappeared: there were no more Austin-Healeys after 1970, for example. The result was a marked degree of demoralisation in the workplace, and this eventually affected the new products that British Leyland was developing.

Meanwhile, major changes were occurring in the sports car's largest market of the USA. In 1965, Ralph Nader published a hugely influential book called *Unsafe at Any Speed*, which openly criticised the US motor industry for ignoring well-founded criticism of its products. Important issues of safety were being ignored, argued Nader, while the car makers focused on cosmetic fripperies that helped to sell cars to customers who knew no better. His book also pointed out that car exhausts were a major factor in creating the air pollution which led to such problems as the smog that blighted the city of Los Angeles.

The book caused a furore, but it also had some far-reaching effects. From 1966, US Federal laws demanded such things as safety padding on instrument panels and safety belts for all the outboard seats in cars. From 1968, US car makers were obliged to meet legally enforceable Federal Motor Vehicle Safety Standards, and the first exhaust emissions control regulations came into force at the same time. Quite reasonably, foreign car-makers who sold their products in America were obliged to conform to the same standards as the domestic manufacturers.

These new standards caused some major headaches for British sports-car makers. Sunbeam stopped making their Alpine not least because it would have been prohibitively expensive to re-engineer it with a fuel tank that met the new US safety standards. The need for safety belts led to quite major and expensive structural changes in some cars. Collapsible steering columns had to be incorporated. Emissions regulations could only be met

From 1967, MG had to redesign the dashboard of its B completely to meet US safety legislation. The huge padded area ahead of the passenger did not incorporate a glovebox, at least initially.

Above: Cost and complication: the additional side marker lights on this 1968 MG Midget MkIII were a further demand of US legislation, as were the head restraints on the seats.

by measures that also reduced engine power and performance, and this in turn impacted on the desirability of sports cars.

All these changes cost money and reduced the profit margins on cars for the USA, as well as introducing unwelcome complication on the production lines. The lower profits inhibited innovation in design, and the constantly tightening safety and emissions regulations tended to make designers reactive rather than proactive. The qualities of rawness and excitement that had once been so important were now largely suppressed as indications of irresponsibility.

All this took the heart out of the British sports car industry, quelling its enthusiasm and leading designers to work within limitations they had never known before. While these limitations undoubtedly made sense in the longer term, the speed with which they were forced on the industry from the end of the 1960s created enormous problems from which the traditional British sports car would never extricate itself. The new designs of the 1970s would be very different indeed, and much the poorer for the change.

FURTHER READING

In a book of this size, it has obviously not been possible to mention every single model of sports car produced by British makers during the 1950s and 1960s. So for those who are interested in finding out more, the following books are recommended reading.

Dymock, Eric. *The MG File*. Dove Publishing, 2001.
Long, Brian. *Daimler V8 SP250*. Veloce Publishing, 1994.
Pressnell, Jon. *Classic British Sports Cars*. Haynes Publishing, 2006.
Pressnell, Jon. *Austin-Healey – The Bulldog Breed*. Haynes Publishing, 2011.
Robson, Graham. *The Triumph TRs, A Collector's Guide*. Motor Racing
    Publications, 1978.
Sedgwick, Michael, and Gillies, Mark. *A–Z of Cars 1945–1970*. Bay
    View Books, 1989.
Taylor, James. *Triumph Spitfire and GT6*. Crowood Press, 2000.

PLACES TO VISIT

Cotswold Motoring Museum & Toy Collection, The Old Mill, Bourton-on-
    the-Water, Gloucestershire GL54 2BY. Telephone: 01451 821255.
    Website: www.cotswoldmotoringmuseum.co.uk
Coventry Transport Museum, Millennium Place, Hales Street, Coventry
    CV1 1JD. Telephone: 024 7623 4270.
    Website: www.transport-museum.com
Haynes International Motor Museum, Sparkford, Yeovil, Somerset BA22 7LH.
    Telephone: 01963 440804. Website: www.haynesmotormuseum.com
Heritage Motor Centre, Banbury Road, Gaydon, Warwickshire CV35 0BJ.
    Telephone: 01926-641188. Website: www.heritage-motor-centre.co.uk
Lakeland Motor Museum, Old Blue Mill, Kendal Road, Backbarrow, Cumbria
    LA12 8TA. Telephone: 01539 530400.
    Website: www.lakelandmotormuseum.co.uk
National Motor Museum, Beaulieu, New Forest, Hampshire SO42 7ZN.
    Telephone: 01590 612345. Website: www.beaulieu.co.uk

Opposite: Triumph replaced the TR5 with the TR6 at the end of the 1960s. Despite a six-cylinder engine, it was still a TR at heart and proved to be a 'heavy-chested' sports car in the mould of the old Austin-Healey 3000.

INDEX